CAUTIONARY CHRONICLES

An Illustrated Compendium
of Human Striving

David Ross Gunn

Fomite
Burlington, VT

Copyright © 2017 by David Gunn

All rights reserved. No part of this book may be reproduced in any form or by any means without the prior written consent, except in the case of brief quotations used in reviews and certain other noncommercial uses permitted by copyright law.

ISBN-13: 978-1-942515-81-4
Library of Congress Control Number: 2016963541

Fomite
58 Peru Street
Burlington, VT 05401
www.fomitepress.com

When Cheerleaders Fell from the Sky

When cheerleaders fell from the sky on that fateful day last June, it was sheer luck that a handful of sure-handed athletes were on hand to catch them. Most of them, anyway.

Lonken-tom Syndroom

Employing complex calculations, Dutch astronomer Christiaan Huygens discovered the rings of Saturn. His brother, Tom, however, used the big telescope for less scholarly purposes: spying on the Szkola Polska women's volleyball team across town. No surprise, really, because the local psychiatrist had already diagnosed his problem as Lonken-tom Syndroom, or Peeping Tom Disorder.

The Diorama

Bernice's Bible studies project was to construct a diorama of the twenty-third Psalm, the one that begins "The Lord is my shepherd; I shall not want." However, a typographical error in the text sent her careening down the wrong path.

In from the Cold

An early version of John LeCarré's best known espionage thriller told the mundane tale of Benny Pringler, who liked to spy on passers-by from his front porch during the spring, summer, and fall, but in the winter came in from the cold and surveilled people from backstage of the Meptang Theater.

Meet the Composer

Wilma's Meet The Composer grant stipulated that she be on hand at the premiere of her commissioned piece, "The Sorcerer's Assistant," to discuss it with the audience. But a lifetime spent in a coven in which the only social activities came from *Grimorium Verum* rituals had limited development of her people skills. Which may be why instead of "interacting" with the attendees, she turned them all into toads.

Big Denny

Big Denny deemed Chez Pringler's frog legs so tasty that he sometimes forgot his table manners and swallowed them whole. Luckily, he was an EMT and knew how to self-administer the Heimlich maneuver by flinging himself down on the floor, face first and hard.

Madge and Badger

In frequency of occurance, Siamese twins are conjoined at the upper chest (28%), thorax (18.5%), lower chest (10%), and nose (1%). Rare, indeed, is it for twins to be attached at the leg (0.008%). Yet that's what befell Madge and Badger Pringler, who overcame that little impediment to become classical ballet dancers. Not *great* ones, you understand, but still ...

Relief from Trismus

Trismus, or lockjaw, refers to a reduced opening of the human jaws caused by a spasm of the muscles of mastication, or, more often, by trying to swallow a small camera. While severely painful, the ailment can often be alleviated by removing the invasive device from one's mouth.

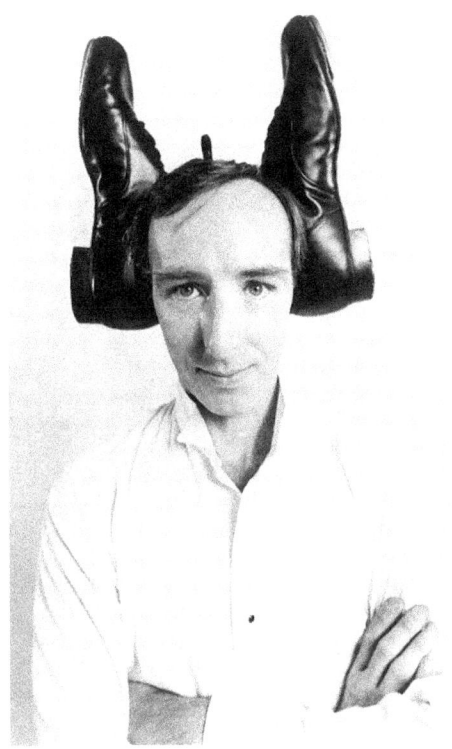

Fred

Fred went to the audiologist complaining of ringing in his ears. After administering a battery of tests, the doctor determined that Fred suffered from Oxforditis, a rare condition in which the sufferer's ears became extended and inverted and smelled of leather. And while that diagnosis did nothing to explain the ringing in Fred's ears, the subsequent discovery of Fred's missing mobile phone in his left ear did.

Human Piñata

No one was more surprised than firefighter Emil Dinklaker when, after supposedly rescuing a middle-aged woman from a burning apartment building, he accidentally bumped her head on an overhanging ledge and it popped off, causing hundreds of toys to erupt from what turned out to be Acme Toys' very lifelike "Blanche, the Human Piñata."

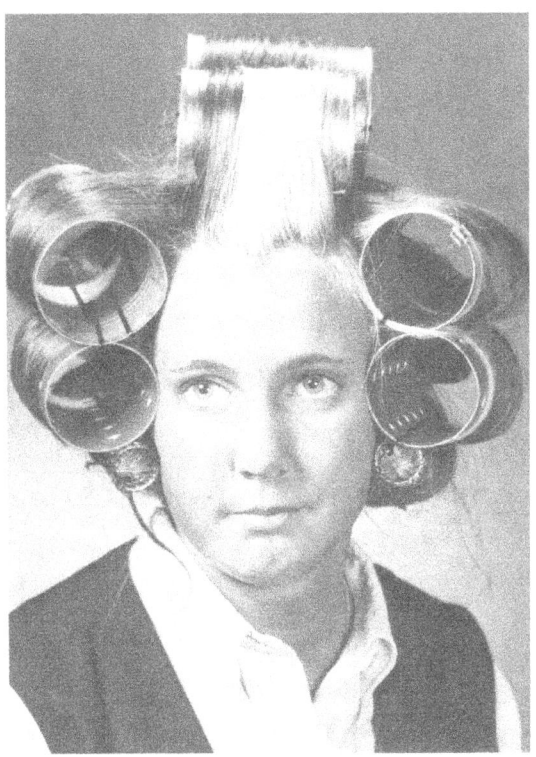

Human Loudspeaker

When Gwendolyn agreed to play the lead role in Dinklaker High School's production of "The Human Loudspeaker," she didn't realize that she'd have to wear six woofers and four tweeters on her head plus carry around a heavy tube amplifier in her pocket. She did enjoy reciting her lines, however, which mostly consisted of a lot of "bzzz-bzzzs" and crackles of static.

The Eyeballotomy

Mimi had had blurry vision for more than a year and the eye baths weren't doing a lick of good. Her optometrist said she needed corneal transplants in both eyes, but when Mimi learned how much they cost, she settled for a cheaper alternative: Dr. Pringler's Outpatient Eyeballotomy, a do-it-yourself procedure that retailed for only $49.95. While the price was right, the operation required nerves of steel. In retrospect, Mimi concedes that she probably shouldn't have tried to save time by performing two eyeballotomies simultaneously directly after she'd enjoyed a double espresso.

Form Follows Function

The "form follows function" principle is hard at work in the Pringler University Library. While books on caves, Death Valley, and boreholes are arrayed on the bottom shelf, Armand Dinklaker's "Illustrated Guide to Gravitational Anomalies, Volume 16: Levitation" is on the very top one.

Incognito

Last year, when Congress slashed the budget of the U.S. Marshals Service, one of the first casualties was the Incognito Division of the Witness Protection Program. Gone, suddenly, were the makeup, wigs, glasses, artificial heads, and other sophisticated appearance-altering devices that helped give new identities to endangered witnesses of crime. In its place was ... well, a recent gathering of currently protected witnesses speaks for itself.

Shoes and Handbags

A frazzled Nurse Wiggins stepped out of the St. Salmon's Hospital's Birthing Center having just assisted her surgical team in a complicated caesarian section on a very expectant Mrs. Gangalore Beetlevue. The operation had resulted in a medical first for the hospital: a baby who resembled a sharply toothed and broadly snouted reptile indigenous to the southeast United States more so than a traditional newborn. Cradling the infant, Nurse Wiggins wondered if the mother's wish to breast-feed was a good idea. What to do?! But then, as Baby X gazed hungrily at her with eyes that harked back to the Oligocene Epoch, the perfect solution came to mind: Shoes! And handbags!

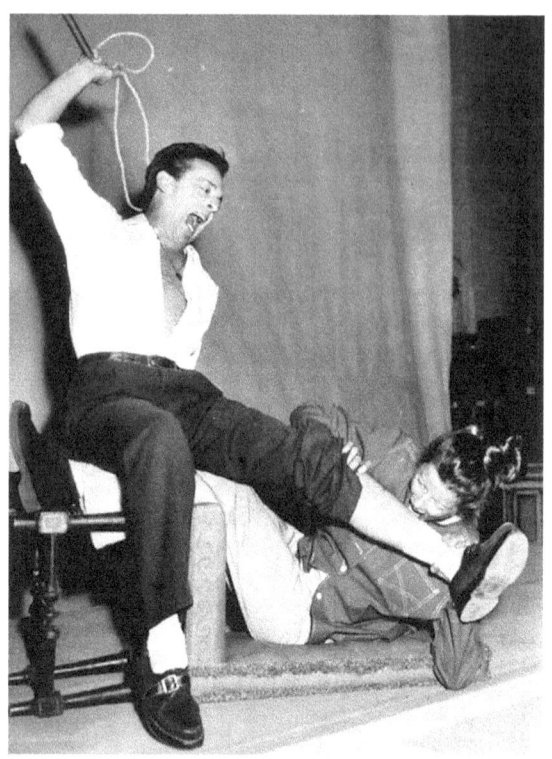

Shinnnnns

As most of us know, zombies of today are propelled by a craving for brains. But in the not too distant past, they favored a lower, more accessible part of their human prey: *shinnnns!*

Berlioz Belles

Symphonie fantastique's final movement is almost never performed as written because Berlioz called for an enormous pair of bells: 18' and 24' in diameter for the C and G bells, respectively. But on August 8, 1998, the Dinklaker Community College Orchestra mounted a performance of the piece that indeed used those big bells. Making the production work were "the Berlioz Belles," members of the college's campanology club seen here in rehearsal. Regrettably, when the conductor cued their entrance, the Belles in their enthusiasm yanked the rope too hard. Both bells broke away from their housing and plummeted onto the instrumentalists who were unluckily seated beneath them, proving that the piece's ending cannot be successfully performed without violas, trombones, oboes, and harps.

Monstrosis

Sam Peckinpah's mayhem-filled 1974 film, "Bring Me the Head of Alfredo Garcia," is based on a much more gruesome tale that involved a kindly watchmaker, his doting wife, and their precocious if troubled young son, Monstrosis.

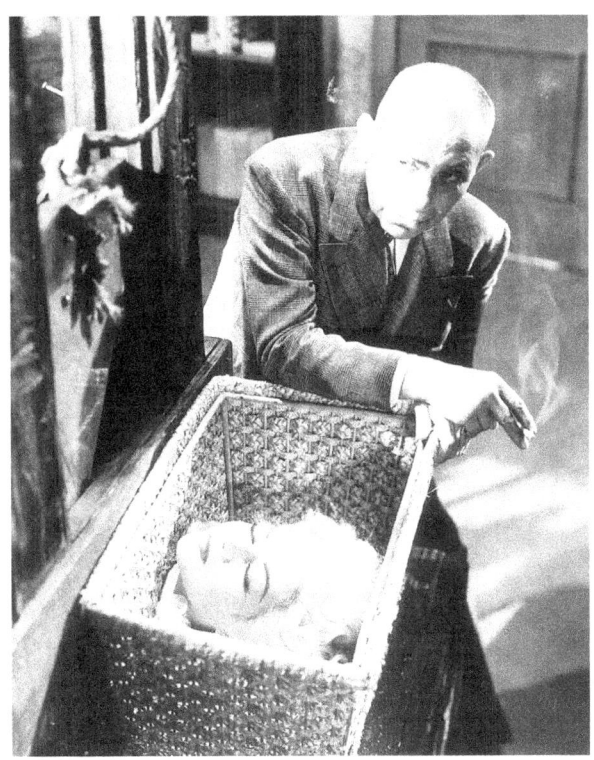

Wrongheadedness

Those *ninnies!* fumed Carl. He'd ordered a head of lettuce from Dinklaker's Gourmet Market. Instead, his delivery parcel contained the head of his company's accounting department. And not for the *first* time, either!

Dinklaker Effect

"That's right, keep them level," cooed Norman, as his charges levitated beach balls over their heads. "No sudden movements now," he cautioned as one woman's ball wobbled slightly in the air. "*Focus*, Blanche!" he cried, but it was too late. The ball suddenly fell heavily to the ground, triggering the Dinklaker Effect, which reversed the positions of the balls and their levitators. But Norman's pupils didn't just hover above their balls. They rose up into the sky, higher and faster, until they disappeared. That was the dark side of the Dinklaker Effect. The good part was that he had first dibs on the contents of the wallets and purses that his erstwhile initiates had left behind. Hmm, not bad. Not bad at all.

Right vs. Wrong

In class today, Lorna learned that there was a right way and a wrong way to have a skin disorder. And, according to her teacher, Lorna had the *right* way. Of course, that didn't make her suppurating cheeks itch any less.

Freefall

One of the wackier dance crazes to hit the U.S. in recent years is the Freefall, inadvertently invented by Esther and Ruby Pringler one evening last January as they attempted to break into their sister-in-law's Miami Beach apartment. Although exceedingly improvisational, the Freefall accurately demonstrates the unencumbered falling motion of a body that is subject only to the earth's gravitational field, one of the four Fundamental Interactions of Nature and the one most likely to give the performer contusions and abrasions.

Acquisition

Publishing giant Random House acquired Dinklaker Millinery Co. with the sole intention of integrating the two disciplines. Success was, er, limited.

On the Steps

"In the Steppes of Central Asia" is a popular tone poem by Russian composer Alexander Borodin that, according to the program notes, "depicts peasants steppe-dancing in the Caucasus outback." However, a recently unearthed photograph of Borodin and his mistress, Inge, captioned "On the steps of the Central Asian Asylum" has fueled speculation that the initial translation was in error.

Valkyrie Sky Ride

Musicologists believe that Richard Wagner got his idea for the beginning of Act 3 of Die Walküre from the Dresden Amusement Park's "Valkyrie Sky Ride," which whirled its shrieking passengers high above the park grounds "like an out of control trip to Valhalla and back," as Wagner himself once described it. Look closely and you'll see him waving from the back of the car while enigmatically dressed as Mrs. A.E. Dinklaker.

Heads and Tubas

People do what they are told not to do. A fundamental tenet of music conservatories, for example, is that "tubas and heads don't mix." Yet hundreds of students get their heads stuck in tubas each year. Is it a rite of passage in the musical world? We asked piano wunderkind Dubois Dinklaker why *he* put a tuba on his head, but he apparently didn't hear the question.

Multi-ductor

Concert audiences today are little impressed by conductors who merely wave their batons at orchestras while providing the occasional showboating gesticulation. That's why the Dinklaker School of Accessory Conducting includes entertainment-oriented courses in its curricula. Legerdemain, ballroom dance, calf roping, hand shadows, ventriloquism, synchronized pie throwing – Dinklaker features them all. Here, Maestro Eugene Pringler multitasks his way through the first movement of Saint-Saëns' "Carnival of the Animals" by conducting, juggling hats, and playing the viola line on a kazoo. He's about to turn around and add the thrilling lion taming component to his performance. Alas, he'll be a split second too late.

Stop the Music

In hindsight, Mayor Pringler admitted that he might have thought of another way to get the high school pep band to stop playing. But more than a hundred people had come to hear him dedicate The World's Largest Slug Farm, and he didn't want them to have to wait around till the band played through its entire repertoire of gastropod-themed songs, all sixty-one of them. Firing a warning shot over the head of the conductor seemed to be the best way to get his attention. And the mayor didn't think that he should be blamed for the misfortune just because his aim was a bit low.

I Piccioni

No one knew why "A Star is Born" attracted such a fervent following of pigeons. In vast numbers they flocked to any cinema where the movie was being screened, only to be turned away by theater managers who, in those days, maintained a strict no-bird policy among theater-goers. So, the birds hung around outside, waiting, sometimes for days on end. The borderline creepiness of the situation did not go unnoticed by rival filmmaker A. J. Hitchcock, who nine years later exploited mankind's innate fear of pigeons in his Italian horror movie, *I Piccioni*. When he made his English language version, however, he wisely re-titled it and toned down the horror to placate squeamish U.S. audiences.

Big Ken

Kurt, Kadeem, Kiefer, Ken, and Konstantin Klagmore were only the second known family of identical quintuplets who lived to adulthood. And yet, when they posed for group photographs, it was hard to see what physical characteristics "Big Ken" shared with his brothers.

Bunnysaurs

The three Bunnysaurs that greeted visitors to Dinklaker Paleontology Institute seemed harmless enough. After all, a computer program limited their animatronics to placid shubbery grazing and cecotrophy. Regrettably, the program failed to suppress the frightful nature of their Triassic Period ancestors in a *fourth* Bunnysaur, whose extirpation of Boy Scout Troop 676 led to a class action lawsuit from which the Institute has yet to fiscally recover.

Statues ≠ Smart

If you want proof that statues are not among the most sharp-witted of inanimate objects, you need only revisit the 1999 All-Species Invitational Diving Competition, held on the campus of the Dinklaker Zoological Research Institute. Although the event lasted from Saturday, June 1, to Tuesday, June 4, the sole statute entry, Bernard Beezer, didn't begin his routine until November 3, 2000, long after the temporary pool facility had been dismantled and shipped back to Coral Gables, Florida.

Dewey's Discombobulation

Library pioneer Melvil Dewey is famous for inventing the Dewey Decimal System of document classification. But the concept didn't come easily to him. He initially preferred the more relaxed system that he had devised while in college.

6'10.5"

At six feet ten and a half inches, Ramona Dinklaker claimed the title of "Tallest Woman in Klondike County," which entitled her to dozens of fabulous prizes. Eventually, however, she was forced to return everything when the runner-up complained that the method of measuring Ramona's height was more than a little suspect.

32 feet per second

From a hundred feet up, it looked to Firefighter Angus Pringler as if he were about to leap into a giant custard pie. Of course, he knew that it was a Browder Life Safety Net, and that he wouldn't pass his fire department's refresher course without jumping onto it. So he stepped across the window threshold. Down, down, down he fell, his fear gradually giving way to a feeling of exhilaration – that is, until he realized that some wisenheimer in the department really *had* substituted a giant custard pie, which, alas, did little to slow his descent of thirty-two feet per second per second.

El Sapo Gordo

The eatery recently voted "Best in the World" by Hearty Trencherman Magazine was Fresno's El Sapo Gordo. Critics gushed over its "refined cuisine, imaginative ideas, and respect for ingredients." That last accolade amused Mrs. Edith Dinklaker, El Sapo Gordo's food buyer, who typically "respected" only ingredients she could find at the local dollar store at half price.

Fat Man

Last week, the American Mycology Federation awarded the title of "World's Biggest Mushroom" to Jerome Dinklaker's "Fat Man," a *boletus fibrillosus* that measured a whopping 5 feet 2 inches from volva to cap. Jerome attributed his mushroom's size to the soil he grew it in, which he'd harvested from the White Sands Missile Range in New Mexico. One of the judges, upon sampling a sliver of stalk, remarked that it "tastes a little like plutonium."

Enid and Larry

Enid was desperate to learn how to dance, but she steadfastly refused to pay the outrageous sum of six bucks an hour for lessons at the Arthur Murray Dance Studio. That's why she wound up at the dollar-a-day Dinklaker School of Terpsichore paired with a passive-aggressive crustacean named Larry, whose only interest in the jitterbug was to try to eat it.

Best Barber in the World

Lloyd Dinklaker boasted that he was the best barber in the world. For sure, he was the most meticulous. He would often spend ten minutes or more measuring a single hair follicle before carefully cutting it. So by the time Lloyd was finished – and satisfied – it was usually time for the client's regularly scheduled follow-up tonsorial treatment.

Lawn Darts, Circa 2015

It was only a matter of time until the erstwhile genteel outdoor game of lawn darts evolved into something more apropos of today's WMD-friendly environment.

Prelude to Guernica

Rags the Tiger was feeling confident as he allowed Dr. Dinklaker to position his head a little to the left. For two hours he had managed to remain absolutely motionless, fooling the doctor and his assistants into thinking he was just another stuffed animal for the museum's African Savanna exhibit. Finally, he could restrain his predator instincts no longer. The subsequent carnage was witnessed by a young museum guide named Pablo Picasso, who later documented it in monochrome for an exhibit at the 1937 World's Fair.

The Warning

WARNING! DO NOT BE CROSSING RIVER WHEN BIRDS ARE FEEDING! said the sign on the bank of Big Pigeon River. But Kusumita was eager to get home, which lay another two miles away, and anyway, she didn't see any birds. The birds, however, saw Kusumita, and when she began to wade across, they rose from a nearby thicket where they had indeed been feeding. Circling above her, they did what birds have for eons done at the conclusion of a hearty meal. Sorry, Kusumita, but you *were* warned!

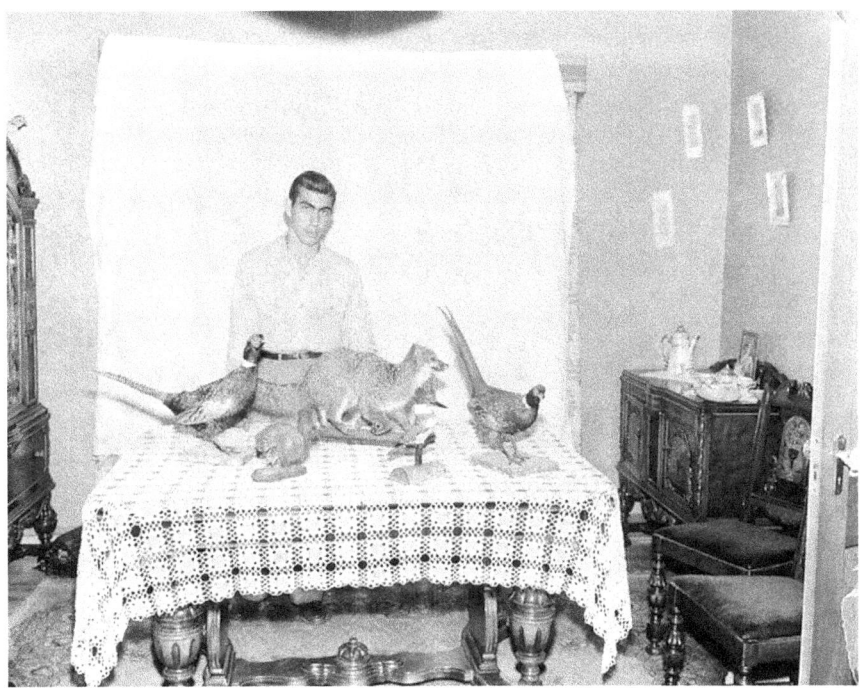

Bob

Enid's taxidermy proficiency was best exemplified by Bob, her first husband. Seated on his favorite chair, his eyes seeming to follow your every move, Bob added a creepy realism to the dining room, an area that Enid's house guests steadfastly avoided.

~~50~~ 60 Rubles

"Fifty rubles to the first peasant, er, *person* who finds my contact lens!" said Ivan Ivanovich Shuysky as he peered nearsightedly at the crowd of people from atop his horse. Although the reward was a fortune in the village of Smootsk, there were no takers. "Hmm," reconsidered the boyar, searching his pants pocket for another coin. "All righty then, make that *sixty* rubles!" That did the trick. At once, the villagers were on their knees, vigorously sifting through soil and gravel. Hours of hard labor passed but no one ever found it, because it was on the kitchen counter where Ivan Ivanovich had dropped it that morning while making oatmeal. If it's any consolation to the villagers, Ivan Ivanovich never found it either, and he remained awkwardly myopic for the rest of his life.

Another Chance

For the ninth straight time, Prescott Pringler scored a perfect 100 on the written part of his driver's license test, but for the ninth straight time, he failed to parallel park properly. Charitably given another chance, he failed on his tenth attempt, too.

The Dowser

At the fifty-second International Dowsers Conference, Mrs. Edna Purdy demonstrates her talent for finding water by using only her fingertips. She was successful in eleven of twelve attempts, and would have been a perfect twelve for twelve if the judges had counted the liquid she located in Mr. Powlaski's colostomy bag.

The Cactus Hat

Although the Pringler Cactus Hat provided superb camouflage for the Lone Ranger when he was tracking outlaws out on the range, it invariably left him with a handful of spines whenever he tipped it to greet the ladies.

Yet Another Chance

When last we heard from Prescott Pringler, he'd failed for the tenth time the parallel parking part of his Missouri driver's license test. Make that eleven times in a row.

The Flamboni Way

Unique in the act of parturition is the Flamboni tribe of northernmost South Africa, where the women bear their young out of the crowns of their heads. They claim that this direct brain-to-birth path gives their offspring a head start in developing vital cognitive abilities. Maybe so, but by bypassing the more traditional uterine preparation chamber, the newborns are more likely to greet the world with anatomical anomalies – and extra legs are *not* out of the question!

Fudge

In its latest issue, Consumer Reports rates the cargo volume of the new four-door Mugu Gaipan at an amazing 172 cubic feet. On closer inspection, however, it turns out that the "amazing" number didn't come without a little fact fudging.

The Birth of the Lightsaber

Contrary to popular belief, the invention of the lightsaber was the result of a series of 18 seemingly unrelated events that ended when Mrs. Millicent Monadnik inadvertently set the focus control of her Dinklaker Duck Defeatherer to "Wide" and her long-suffering husband, Lars, suffered one last time by somehow becoming a 1.33-meter-long blade of plasma.

Atilla's Gastronomic Legacy

During his fearsome reign, Attila the Hun plundered much and killed many. Yet today, his rampant brutality is excused, thanks to his gastronomic legacy. Attila had a sweet tooth, and after pillaging the countryside, he liked nothing better than to relax in his tent with a bowl of sugary treats. One day, when his fanatical followers interrupted his respite by saluting him with flaming torches, Attila's temper got the better of him and he irately flung a bowl of marshmallows at them. Always battle ready, the men instinctively caught the confections on the ends of their torches. The result: the toasted marshmallow, which is still enjoyed today *après le combat*.

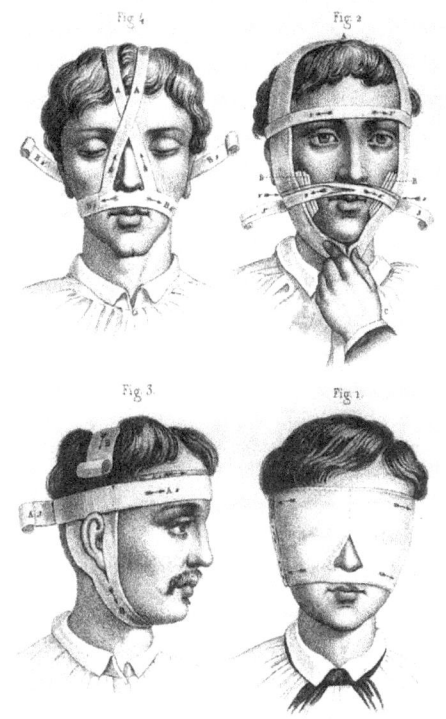

The Model 5

Elmer P. Dinklaker Milliners, Ltd., revolutionized the headgear industry when it introduced a line of hats that stayed put on the wearer's head even under the windiest of conditions. A simple harness that anchored hat to head with a minimum of fuss made the Model 5 a huge success. The same could not be said, however, for Models 1 through 4, though the Model 2 did enjoy a brief period of notoriety when it appeared in a retrospective of the accoutrements of the Marquis de Sade.

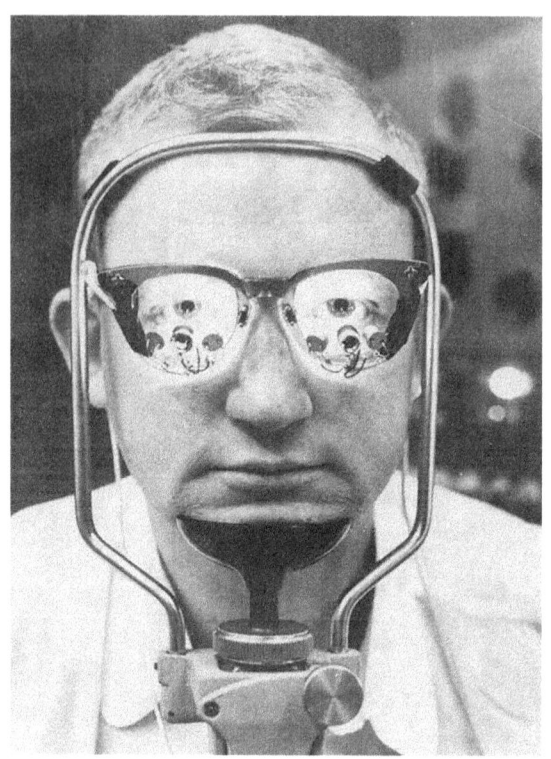

The Mark VI

The Dinklaker Mark VI Deluxe Reading Glasses featured six tiny lamps designed to illuminate an object in front of the wearer. And while the concept was sound, the product still needed some fine-tuning before it was ready to "revolutionize the consumer spectacles industry."

The Rhinotillexisicist

Miriam was a poised, professional woman who unfortunately suffered from rhinotillexis, or the act of nose picking. For hours at a time, in went the finger, out came the dried nasal secretions. She just couldn't stop herself! A therapist advised Miriam to find something else to occupy her hands and recommended the South Indian classical dance known as Bharatanatyam, whose hand movements are both multifarious and complex. Miriam did so, and got quite good at it. Still, every so often, she would catch her fingers straying towards those ever so inviting nasal orifices, *aaaargh!*

The Suppositor

Patients at St. Salmon's Hospital—such as Giuseppe, here—hated it when Nurse Beaufort was on duty because she always eschewed suppositories in favor of a "hands-on" procedure.

The Great Malaxo

 Pick a card, any card!" said The Great Malaxo confidently. "But I don't *see* any cards!" countered Amy as she groped blindly about her. Malaxo fanned the cards in front of her face, but to no avail. She apparently still couldn't see them. "Hmm," he muttered, "I seem to be missing some crucial component of this trick!" So, not for the first time, it was back to the drawing board for the now only *occasionally* great prestidigitator.

The Record

More than anything, Ernestina Dinklaker wanted to be listed in the Guinness Book of World Records. For two years, she thought long and hard about what unique skill she possessed that would grant her that status. In the end, a healthy bladder determined the category: "Biggest Clean Catch Sample Provided for a Urinalysis." Ernestina's yield of 3.728 quarts won easily.

Leave it to Cleaver

"Leave it to Beaver" was a family-oriented situation comedy of the 1960s. Its earliest episodes, however, were of a darker nature as they documented the life of Beaver Cleaver's aunt, Carrie, a troubled woman who had a penchant for turning her surname into a verb.

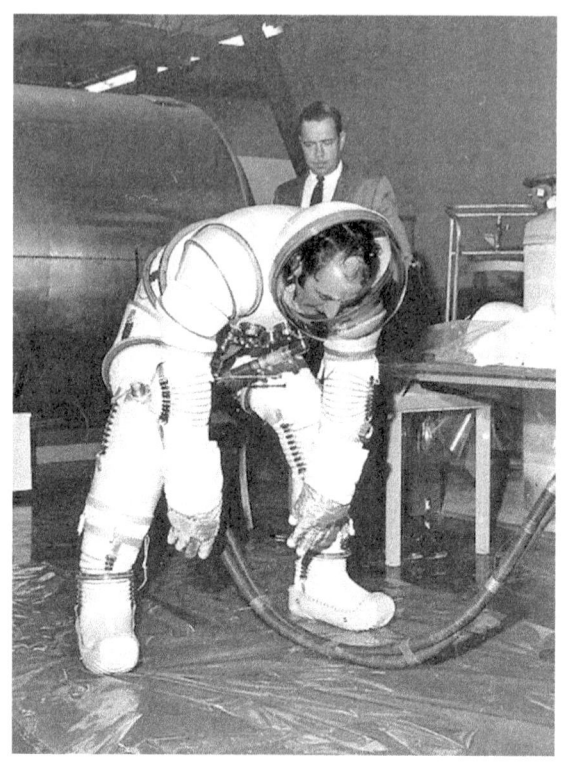

Rule 15: Do Not Yodel

As his extravehicular mobility unit swiftly lost pressure, compromising its hermetical seal, astronaut Clive Dinklaker remembered again why it was so hazardous to yodel while suited up.

Valet Parking

Whenever Brad landed his Piper Cub at a new airport, he always paid a little extra to have his aircraft valet-parked. But that "little extra" didn't extend as far as tipping the taxiway pilot, a slight that would come back to haunt him at Meptang Regional Airport, where valet parker Patel Pringler clearly showed his annoyance.

Ursine Valet Parking

Attendance at Yellowstone National Park shot way up after the park introduced ursine valet parking. "Our bears will park your car for you – and you never have to tip 'em!" crowed Park Superintendent Pringler. Of course, the bears weren't great drivers, and more than one coupé wound up in a ditch by the side of the road. But Pringler put a positive "adventure in nature" spin on these incidents, and visitor traffic actually increased. That all changed when a grizzly bear was tabbed to park an RV but ate the driver and his family instead. Even *that* PR nightmare might've been minimized if a home movie of the gruesome kill hadn't gone viral.

The Long Rue

The photographer again asked old Mother Morris if she was ready to have her picture taken, emphasizing that he was at the end of his roll of film and they likely wouldn't have another chance. Striking a thoughtful pose, Mother Morris said that, yes, she was ready. But then at the last moment the poor woman had one of those inexorable digit-to-nose urges, well knowing it would result in a portrait that she would long rue.

Les Flambeaux

Bernard was a good juggler but not a *great* one, a limitation that was painfully evident when he attempted to juggle the flaming torches, or les flambeaux.

The Beulah

Lost among the annals of Christopher Columbus' 1492 voyage to the New World is the fact that he left Spain with *four* ships – the Niña, the Pinta, the Santa Maria, and the Beulah. The nearer they got to the edge of the world, however, the more anxious the Beulah's skipper became. So one night when a blanket of fog hid the Beulah from the other vessels, he turned south towards what he thought was safety. Unfortunately he sailed straight to the land of Brobdingnag and ran aground on Lady Patience Zargogwy as she was enjoying her morning swim.

Nexus

Even for Nexus, one of the longest enduring professional percussion ensembles in the world, times were tough. Performance opportunities were down and paid considerably less than in the good old days when thousands of spectators regularly packed their concerts. Which is why its members jumped at the chance to participate in the first annual Butterball Turkey Parade and Skeet Shoot down King Street in Toronto. Nexus augmented the traditional complement of marching drums with marimbas, tam tams, and a wind machine. While the battery of additional instruments was indeed impressive to look at, their relative immobility doomed them as they suffered the brunt of the falling debris when an overeager skeet shooter blasted the giant helium-filled turkey piñata out of the sky.

A Relative Term

The notion that earwigs burrow into the brains of humans through the ear and lay their eggs there had long been attributed to superstition. But then "Lucky" Ernest Pringler showed up at the Mayo Clinic with a dazed look on his face. After a cursory examination, a team of creeped-out otorhinolaryngologists removed a female earwig from Ernest's left ear and these 287 eggs from his right. Ernest remains dazed to this day, so I guess "lucky" is a relative term.

Cloak and Dagger

Nowadays, a spy can easily dispose of a secret message he's received just by pressing the Erase button on his telephone answering machine or, in the case of email, the Delete key on his computer. But not so long ago, covert communications were often entrusted to vinyl records. And they didn't burn, they wouldn't fit in a garbage disposal, and most creditable spook organizations considered burying them in rabbit warrens a security risk. What to do? Agent Bob's solution, while effective, has yet to catch on.

Jack and Jill

Intending to fetch a pail of water, Jack and Jill went up the hill, where they were greeted by a stagnant pool from which iridescent plumes of noxious vapors arose. Jack dared Jill to drink the water. When Jill refused, Jack called her a sissy, scooped up a handful, and drank the tangy liquid. Later, back at the playground at the bottom of the hill, a contrite Jack had reason to rue his rash act.

Worse than Hives

Early telephones were vectors for virulent germs, and until the nascent telecommunications disinfectant industry pressed into service the first wave of telephone sanitizers, many users suffered painful rashes, hives, and worse.

First Transistor Radio

The first transistor radio had a major design flaw. While it was indeed pocket-sized, its antenna weighed 200 pounds and required continuous tinkering from an electrical engineer. Sales flagged until a clever company advertiser repurposed the device as a piñata.

Hypocrisy

After John Carlos and Tommie Smith raised their arms in a Black Power salute following their podium finish at the 1968 Olympics' 200 meter race, they were expelled from the Games and harshly ostracized. But two days later, when Rose, Gertrude, Zeppelina, and Lois struck nearly the identical pose after creaming the competition in the Dinky Duck Slip 'n Slide Relay, the same panel of judges saw only "four cute little cut-ups."

The Bartered Bride

The Manayunk Opera Company's new production of "The Bartered Bride" takes a few liberties with Bedřich Smetana's masterpiece. For example, the setting is moved from mid-19th century Prague to Bloomer, Kansas, a hundred years later. That switch makes it more credible for the bride, Mařenka, to be bartered for a 1953 Pontiac Chieftain instead of a sizable dowry for her parents. In this scene, Mařenka sings the aria "You call this 'mint condition'?! You're nuts!" – emphasizing her displeasure by stomping her foot, regrettably on the instep of Kecal the marriage broker.

Jungle Cruise

When the Disneyland theme park opened in Anaheim, California, a popular ride was to have been the Jungle Cruise. But due to an administrative error, the designer, Bob, built a replica of the Great Dayton, Ohio, Flood of 1913. It was bad enough that riders had to sit in uncomfortable wooden boats as they floated past 20,000 life-sized flood-devastated homes, but when they entered the lagoon that contained the carcasses of 1,200 drowned horses, their patience finally ended – as did, not surprisingly, Bob's tenure with Disneyland.

Using his Head

Last year, house razing projects in Conchoid County were few and far between, causing Dinklaker Demolition to miss six consecutive payments on its business loan. Hence, the bank had no option but to repossess the company's D4K XL bulldozer. So when a demolition job finally did materialize, company president Daryl Dinklaker personally dealt with the missing equipment issue.

Perfect Timing

'Mmm-mmm,' thought Joe Bob dreamily, 'there's just nuthin' that goes with an ice cold Perky Cola like fresh pigeon-on-a-stick!' And since Joe Bob already had the Perky Cola and he also had the stick, all he needed was a ... whoa! If his eyes did not deceive him, he was right now starin' at one heck of an instance of perfect timing.

The Distraction

Tryouts for the SEALs were among the most rigorous in the entire U.S. Naval Special Warfare arena. To test each candidate's aptitude for concentration – key to the success of any mission – the panel of judges would typically add a "distraction" to the audition.

The Rats in the Walls

When Howard Lovecraft's short story, "The Rats in the Walls," was published in 1923, it was only a modest success. However, its gothic horror seemed perfectly suited to the wide screen, so plans were made to film it. More than two thousand professional rat actors were hired, and soon the sound stage was crawling with human vermin. Determined to stay in character, they promptly spread plague throughout the studio while eating the producer and best boy. Finding the walls in which they were supposed to lurk in the film too confining, they commandeered the entire studio lot, including the famous Paramount Theater, where, it's rumored, their progeny can still be found today.

Caveat Emptor

Boyer World Airlines offered the cheapest coast-to-coast passenger fares by far, often undercutting competing air carriers by 90 percent. But you get what you pay for. Or in Boyer Air's case, you *don't* get the seat that you didn't pay for.

The Higgs Boson

For half a century, scientists had searched for the Higgs boson, a hypothetical elementary particle purported to be an integral component of the material world. To confirm its existence, physicists had conducted thousands of complex experiments at research laboratories such as CERN in Switzerland and Fermilab in Illinois, but to no avail. So imagine their surprise when farmer Orestes P. Dinklaker announced that, no big deal, he had a Higgs boson in his backyard chained to a tree "'cuz," he drawled, "it's a danged squirrelly subatomic particle."

The Birdbath

Emil was simply beside himself when he discovered how fragile his new electronic birdbath was. Why, he no more than sneezed in its general direction and the darned thing toppled over, hit the ground, and shattered. At least the robin that had been drinking at the time—which, insisted Emil, was *this big*—escaped with only a minor shrapnel wound.

Etch a Sketch: The Early Years

Before a 90% cut to the manufacturing budget translated into a substantially smaller product, the Etch A Sketch mechanical drawing toy measured 80 by 120 feet and required three automobiles, their drivers, and a mechanical engineer to operate.

Bye-bye, Brad

What puts the massive Convention Hall Auditorium Pipe Organ in Atlantic City, N.J., in a class by itself is its 184-foot long Diaphone Basso Profunda, a pipe so big that even the 41,000 seat auditorium can't accommodate it. Instead, the pipe exits through a hole in the west wall of the mezzanine and empties at the base of the building near a "Beware Of Loud Sounds" sign. A local middle school science teacher once theorized that air pressure from the business end of the pipe created a powerful mesovortex, but he didn't know *how* powerful. Could it, say, launch a relentlessly misbehaving fourth grade pupil named Brad three blocks to the ocean? As he sat down at the organ console, both he and Brad were about to find out.

Wynken, Blynken, and Nadine

The three aliens, Wynken, Blynken, and Nadine, had been on Earth for nearly a year before they were discovered. They had agreed to be part of an amateur fashion show at the high school they had infiltrated. But as they strolled down the runway, one of the spotlights shorted out, causing a temporal rift to suddenly open up directly above them and play havoc with their gravitational anchors. As the three sister-pods rose into the air, they sensed their roles as clandestine extraterrestrial observers coming to an abrupt end.

Catch it if you Can

"Quick! Throw me another one!" shouted Jeff. He had already caught and stacked twelve TVs as the "Catch It If You Can!" audience hollered words of encouragement. Fourteen TVs was the record, and Jeff was sure he could break it and win the grand prize. Regrettably, the thought distracted him just as Bruno, the show's pitcher, lobbed the 26" Philco double-door console. The audience sighed a collective "aww" as they didn't get to see the record broken. On the other hand, most of Jeff *was*.

Myrna

'I have to go out of town tomorrow,' he says. 'Could you come over to my house and feed Myrna?' he says. 'And maybe take her out of her cage so she can run around a bit?' he says. 'Or just hold her for a minute or two since she really likes to cuddle?' he says. Well, if *that* was her idea of cuddling, I'd hate to see her when she's overwrou ... "*Back*, Myrna, *get ba ... aaiiiiyy!*"

The Fightin' Narwhals

The annual All-Wales Swimming Competition offers teams around the country a chance to show off their natatorial talents. Here, the Ystradgynlais Constabulary Fightin' Narwhals regrettably lose beaucoup points during their Synchronized Water Entry portion of the contest.

The Medusa Effect

Members of the Wisenheimer Metropolitan Police were hot on the trail of Hank E. Panké, the notorious mountebank who had evaded capture for more than a year. The first constable who discovered him, however, had not been apprised of Panké's ability to turn adversaries to stone with one withering gaze, and his colleagues came upon poor Chauncey after he'd already been immobilized by the Medusa Effect. And because no one knew how to reverse the Effect, Chauncey wound up with all the other unfortunates in the sculpture garden behind Police Headquarters.

Get Down

In the late 1960s, guitarist Carlos Santana's idea of fusing Latin rhythms with rock 'n' roll ran into a major obstacle: he didn't have any money to hire musicians. His wealthy father sure did, but he wouldn't loan Carlos a dime unless he featured his aunts Benadrilio and Darvonilla in the band. But their addition to the percussion section proved providential as their ability to "get down" always met with audience approval.

The Champion Cartwheeler

World champion speed cartwheeler Imogene Dinklaker prepared for each of her competitions the same way: by racing the westbound 20th Century Limited passenger train – right up to the day that she encountered an unexpectedly *east*bound train.

Taxiing and Parking

After he aced the written part of the Airline Transport Pilot test, Bob was feeling pretty cocky, a feeling that lasted only until he embarked on the hands-on segment titled "Taxiing and Parking."

Show and Tell Day

Lucille bragged that she had the world's biggest ant farm, but she bragged about lots of things so her classmates didn't believe her. That changed when she brought it to school for Show and Tell Day. And when one of the critters escaped from the enclosure, she learned firsthand that bigger was not always better, especially when bigger also meant "carnivorous."

Shingle Shortage

During the horrific and still unexplained shingle shortage of 1989, roofers around the world often had to come up with innovate ways to complete their building projects. (Note: "Innovative" did not always mean "successful.")

Shuffleboard: The Beginning

The game of shuffleboard began life when chef Elvira Dinklaker tried to cook up a batch of biscuits in a giant frying pan for her realty TV show. An assistant had incorrectly set the temperature of the oversized stove to High, which caused the batter to stick to the pan. In her struggle to loosen the sizzling glop, Elvira pushed too hard on the spatula, sending the biscuit-to-be shooting out into the studio, where it clobbered an annoying heckler. The delighted crowd cheered, awarding Elvira 10 points. Standardized scoring and team jerseys followed soon thereafter.

Disneyland: The Beginning

According to theme park lore, Walt Disney came up with the idea of Disneyland after visiting various amusement parks in the 1930s and 1940s. But his lifelong love of rides started much earlier: the day his ma brought home a road kill deer and his pa attached it to the family swing set. You can still see what's left of the swing set near the end of Mr. Toad's Wild Ride in the Anaheim theme park."

Where's Hamish?

It was embarrassing enough when Hamish accidentally fell into the toaster and then couldn't get back out. It was even worse, though, when his mother had to extricate him with help from the bloody Hoover.

The Knitter

Professional knitter Eloise Dinklaker takes her work very seriously. So when the Rangoon Times' weaving critic assailed one of her elegant intarsias as "a stitcher's worst nightmare," she threw up her hands in disgust. Unfortunately for the critic, who was standing nearby, her hands were chock-full of the tools of her trade.

Ol' Squinty

William Tell once famously shot an apple off of the head of his son with a bolt from his trusty crossbow. Sure, Tell, a celebrated marksman, was known for his unerring accuracy. But *un*known to the public were the dozens of his assistants – such as Leonard here – who, over the years, made the ultimate sacrifice as Ol' Squinty ever so slowly improved his aim.

Crickets

Long considered to be one of the most boring competitive sports ever invented, the game of cricket got a welcome infusion of excitement one spring day in 2014 when Dr. Dagmar Dinklaker released a pair of giant carnivorous cricket-bots onto the playing field.

The Boy who Walked on Water

During the early twentieth century, Edwin Pringler was known throughout England as "The Boy Who Walked on Water" because that's what he did. Still, it was odd that no one ever questioned the helium-filled balloons tethered to his head that seemed to provide the necessary buoyancy.

Two Measures Early

J.D. Pringler's avant-garde tour de force "Hurl" called for a chorus of 70 children to vigorously expectorate at the piece's climax. Regrettably, little Leslie Banglobber came in two whole measures early, ruining the surprise moment.

When GPS Units go Bad

"Turn left, *turn left!*" shrieked Juliet. "But the GPS unit says to go straight!" argued Romeo. "So straight ahead we'll gooooooooooooooo ..." "*Aiyeeee!*" commented Alice and Bob.

102

Albuminoid Pingo Dingback

Photographer Margaret Bourke-White was renowned for being the first American female war photojournalist. But equally important was her pioneering of the Albuminoid Pingo Dingback, a technique of pressing the camera shutter release with the photographer's prehensile foot so as to free up her hands for more important activities. When she applied for a patent on the technique, Bourke-White's explanation for the name was "Well, it's bleedin' obvious, isn't it?"

Sabre Dance

For years, the original version of Aram Khachaturian's "Sabre Dance" was not performed by American symphony orchestras because the Occupational Safety and Health Administration found the finale to be unduly hazardous. But in today's economically severe environment, spectacle trumps safety. Hence, the lively tune as Aram envisioned it is more likely to appear on a concert program, no matter the often dire consequences that befall the sacrificial percussionist.

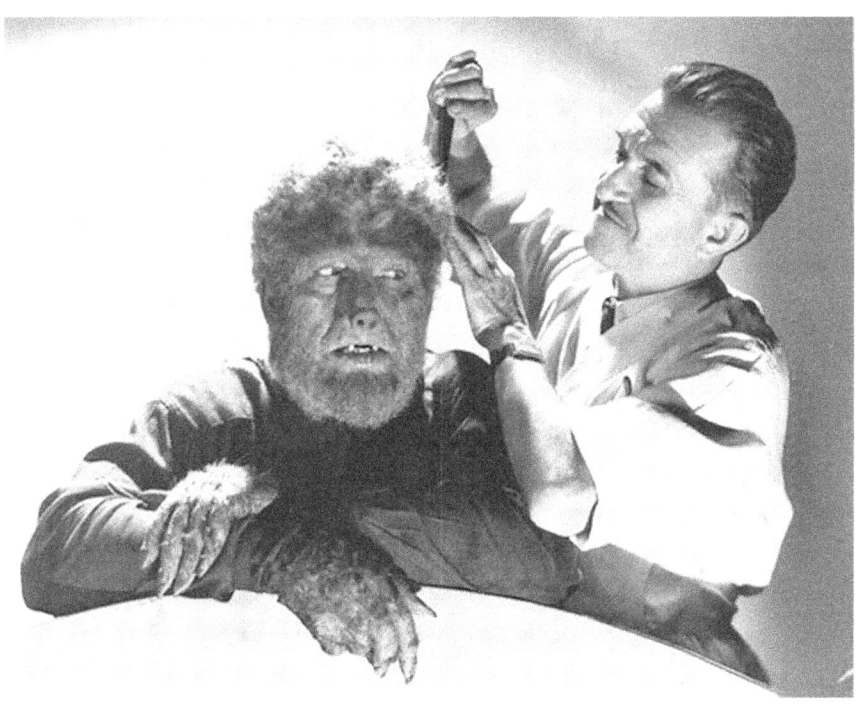

At the Hair Stylist

Many humans harbor a deep-seated fear of werewolves, but the same is true of werewolves – they're scared to death of humans! Or at least the ones who tend to their hair care needs. And lycanthropes have a lot of hair care needs. Whether they're in for their weekly trim or a once-a-month pedicure, werewolves *hate* having their fur touched, even by a caring professional. Now, this is usually more worrisome for the hair stylist, for while the werewolf may suffer the fleeting ignominy of an unattractive coif, the stylist will typically wind up with his viscera ripped out, greatly diminishing the employee's productivity.

The Manicurist

Barbie was the only manicurist at the Henny Penny Hair Salon who agreed to work on the hands of snooty old Mrs. Rosencrantz, but she drew the line when the crone demanded a pedicure.

Escape from Alcatraz

The 1979 American film "Escape from Alcatraz" was based on the true story of the notorious Dinklaker sisters who, in 1967, managed to squeeze through the bars of their prison cell door, overpower the guard, steal the RMS Queen Mary, which had unexpectedly docked at the island pier, and escape, never to be seen again – except, decades later, in the occasional company of Elvis.

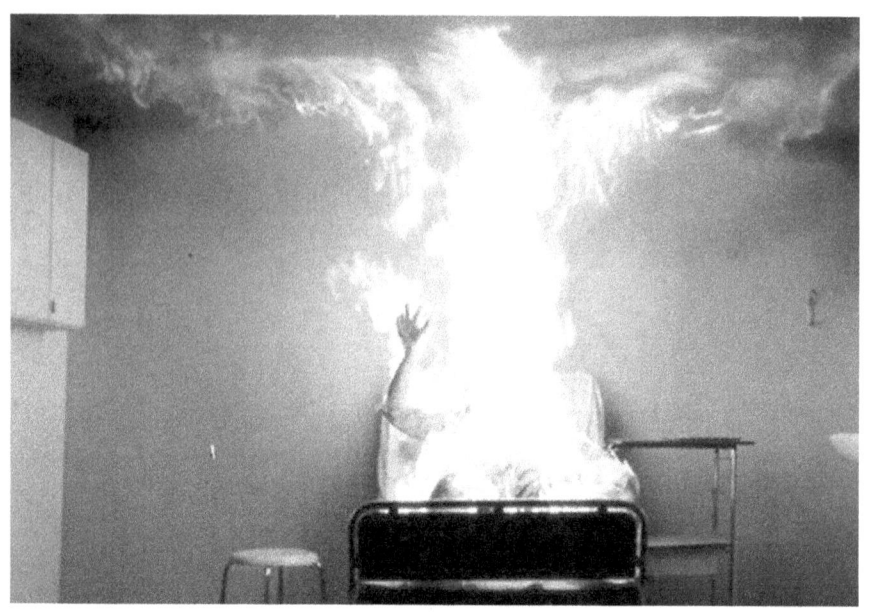

Acuto Vasomotor Flush

"Doctor!"
"Nurse?"
"Mrs. Dinklaker has taken a turn for the worse!"
"I see. And what are her symptoms?"
"Acute vasomotor flushes."
"Vaso what?"
"She is experiencing severe hot flashes, doctor."
"Oh, that. It's a menopause thing, right? Everybody gets them. Every woman, that is. No need to worry."
"Begging your pardon, doctor, but Mrs. Dinklaker's latest flush is unusually severe."
"She's my patient. And I say she's perfectly all ri ... say, what's that awful noise?"
"It's the smoke detector. In Room 4."

The Sunken Cathedral

Claude Debussy initially wanted his piano prelude "The Sunken Cathedral" to be performed in a church at the bottom of a lake. To prove that it could be done, Claude spent hours practicing the piece underwater in a diving suit. Although he was able to hit all of the right notes, the sheet music tended to drift away from him. So he hired Mimi Dinklaker, a professional page-turner who owned a Rouquayrol regulator. But then he discovered his piano was naturally buoyant; it wouldn't stay put underwater. And when he lined the piano with cement blocks to keep it from floating to the surface, it went sharply out of tune. Debussy finally gave up on an *in situ* premiere, though he did *pretend* to play it during the summer of 1912 when he was Sea World of Paris's Guest Artist.

The Welcome Wagon

Welcome Wagon, the world's largest greeting service to the new homeowner, got off to a rocky start when, due to an administrative error, its first hires included the Younger Brothers, Jesse and Frank James, and a misanthropic Matthew "Ace" Nelson, who plugged Bob, Bernice, and Benny Baluchi, the family they were supposed to be welcoming.

PSIS

The Pringler School of Integrated Studies claims that skills its students learn in one discipline can easily be applied to another, no matter how dissimilar the two may seem to be. And it's true! Thelma, here, is leagues ahead of her dental hygiene classmates, thanks to a hands-on technique she learned in Carpentry 101 from PSIS.

NIMBY

Emil Dinklaker's initial proposal for a wind farm comprised five turbines on 30 acres of land adjacent an abandoned railroad spur on the edge of town. The land had long lain fallow, so Emil figured he was putting it to good use. He had not, however, figured on the small but vocal group of NIMBY – or Not In My Back Yard – opponents. So he scaled back his project. Not once or twice but *eight* times, until the design that ultimately won approval from the grumpy protestors didn't even rely solely on wind as its energy source!

The Marshmallow King

Aloysius Pringler's sole claim to fame was that he could eat a roasted marshmallow without having to wait for it to cool down. You might think that this wasn't anything to write home about. And, in fact, Aloysius never did mention it in his numerous letters to his parents in which he asked for money to pay for his law school studies—studies that invariably took a back seat to his marshmallow eating escapades.

Ring Around the Collar

In 1977, Lloyd Dinklaker's "You've got ring around the collar!" laundry detergent jingle became one of the best known slogans in advertising history. But Lloyd's inspiration didn't come from spotting a dirty shirt collar one day. Rather, it came from his son, Benson, who tended to parade around the house clad in ... well, you can guess.

Make a Wish

The wishbone has long been a symbol of good luck: Two people each grab hold of one side of the chicken bone and pull it till it breaks. The one with the longer half gets her wish. But when Libby and Leona tried it, they didn't know that it only worked if the bone was already out of the chicken.

Wishful Thinking

Dinklaker Explosives Cleanup and Containment was highly regarded in the hazardous materials disposal industry for its unblemished safety record until that fateful day when the company outsourced a simple bomb disposal detail to a temporary agency whose attention to detail proved to be only wishful thinking.

Flossing

Large animal dental hygienist Lorna Dinklaker was forever urging her clients to floss properly, but their lack of opposable thumbs made it difficult for them to even hold a toothbrush. So she was resigned to do it for them at their annual check-ups, no matter their halitosis was so overpowering that she sometimes fainted at the most inopportune times.

Heimlich's Maneuver

During a heated debate long ago, Mesopotamian politician Hammurabi Heimlich spontaneously invented the Heimlich maneuver as he tried to rid the parliament of an "obstructing foreign body" named Achilles.

Poor Angus

Corporal Angus Dinklaker of the Queen's Guard had a very sensitive nose. Tea Biscuit, Her Majesty Queen Elizabeth II's horse, had frequent bouts of flatulence that were positively mephitic. Last Monday afternoon, the two universes collided. Poor Angus!

The Venus Dresstrap

To prove he did have a sense of humor, Calvin Klein once designed the Venus Dresstrap. Modeled after the Venus flytrap subtropical plant, the Dresstrap similarly trapped and, over the course of two days, ate its wearer.

Fire!

According to the American Conflagration Association, the most perilous part of fighting fires occurs when the alarm sounds, because it's human nature for everybody in the fire house to race to get down the pole first.

The Spitting Image

When Bernice told Earl that the bust the she had carved was "the spitting image" of him, he assumed she meant that it would, you know, *resemble* him. So he was disappointed to discover that it was intended for his back yard where it would "spit" water all over his wretched petunias.

The Re-Match

The first time that Goliath faced David (1 Samuel, chapter 17), David KOed his bigger foe with a sling, some stones, and a lot of attitude. But in subsequent rematches, Goliath trounced David. *Every* time.

Extemporaneous Urban Forager

Extemporaneous Urban Forager LuAnn Dinklaker spent her days rummaging through the city's commercial trash receptacles for discarded treasures. Her only bad experience was the time she reached for a paper clip at the bottom of a recycling bin on Blighter Street, lost her balance, and then was unable to move for half a day until the earth rotated 180 degrees on its axis. When the ground turned upside down again, LuAnn fell out of the bin, dazed, but still clutching her hard-won prize.

Mr. Television

During the 1950s and '60s, Milton Berle was known to millions of TV viewers as Mr. Television. Sure, as host of NBC's Texaco Star Theatre, he was the first major American television star, but there was more to it than that.

The '79 Nova
Although the 1979 Chevy Nova had more than its share of mechanical problems, everyone agreed that its heater was positively top of the line.

Zarpox

Zarpox and his assistant, Bill, were on Earth to coordinate a massive invasion from Mars. Bill had assumed conventional human form while Zarpox adopted the guise of a familiar mouth accessory. Bill infiltrated the U.S. Department of Defense by sweet-talking Betty, one of its secretaries, into allowing him access to sensitive research files. As Bill figured out how to systematically neutralize America's entire security network, Zarpox radiated his excitement. Regrettably, his "excitement" smelled a lot like burning tobacco. And to a fiercely anti-smoking crusader like Betty, that spelled trouble for Zarpox.

I ♥ What?!

In an attempt to drum up business in a sluggish economy, the Dinklaker Institute of Visual Language printed a thousand glossy brochures that extolled the many benefits of attending the school. Its facts and figures were impressive, indeed. However, the image on the cover bewildered more than a few would-be matriculants, for it spelled out in American Sign Language "I ♥ Smegma."

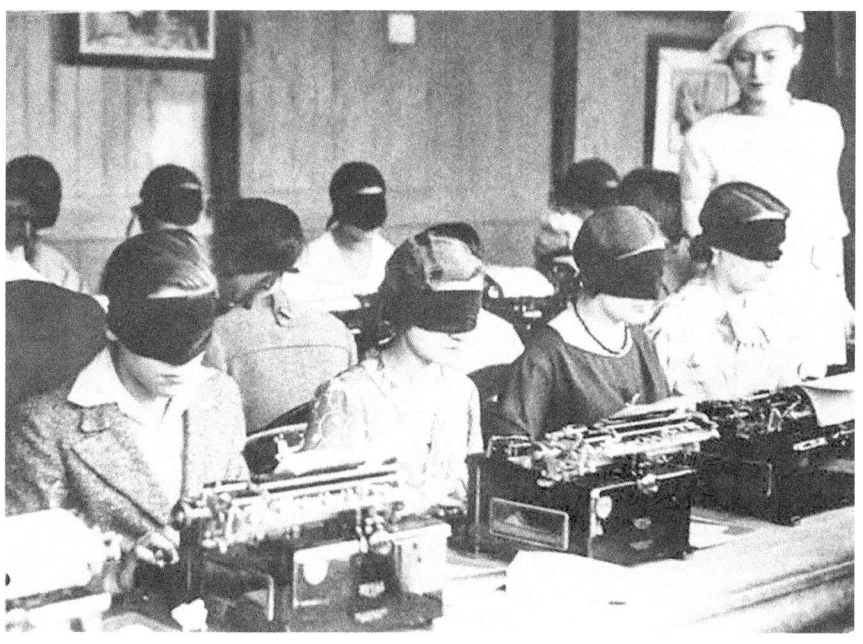

Attention to Detail

For years, the Henny Penny Typewriter Service had been voted the county's best copying company. The meticulous attention to detail of its dedicated staff typically resulted in flawless transcriptions. That all changed when a conjunctivitis epidemic swept through the workplace. To limit contagion, the company nurse prescribed warm compresses over the eyes of the affected employees. Which was, unfortunately, all of them.

The Blade-o-Buick

Lost among other Dallas, Texas, tragedies of November 22, 1963, was the debut of the "Blade-o-Buick" at the Tenth International Housewares Show. The revolutionary food processing appliance's powerful whirling blade created an unanticipated mesovortex that sucked eight unlucky onlookers into the machine's maw, an incident so grim that even the finest spin doctors of the day were unable to sugarcoat it.

The Riesenklavier

Esteemed pianist Andre Dinklaker had always yearned for a Bösendorfer Riesenklavier, reputed to be the biggest piano in the world, thanks to the extra trill octave. And one day, he found it – in, of all places, his neighboring town of Pringlerville! Andre was on tour when it was delivered, so he was as surprised as anyone when he got home and discovered that not only was the Riesenklavier the world's biggest piano, it was also the heaviest.

Huitzilopochtli
Blanche, Mindy, and Cindy modeled their root beer stand after the head of Huitzilopochtli, an Aztec god and patron of the city of Tenochtitlan. But that decision came back to haunt them when the head abruptly came to life and left no doubt as to why Huitzilopochtli was also known as the Aztec god of Human Sacrifice.

The Once Consummate Waitress
For 20 years, Lorelei was The Dinklaker Diner's consummate waitress. But eventually, business flagged, the diner closed, and Lorelei retired to the Old Waitresses Home. You can find her there today, usually sitting in the garden, staring vacantly into the distance while still trying to refill that customer's water glass.

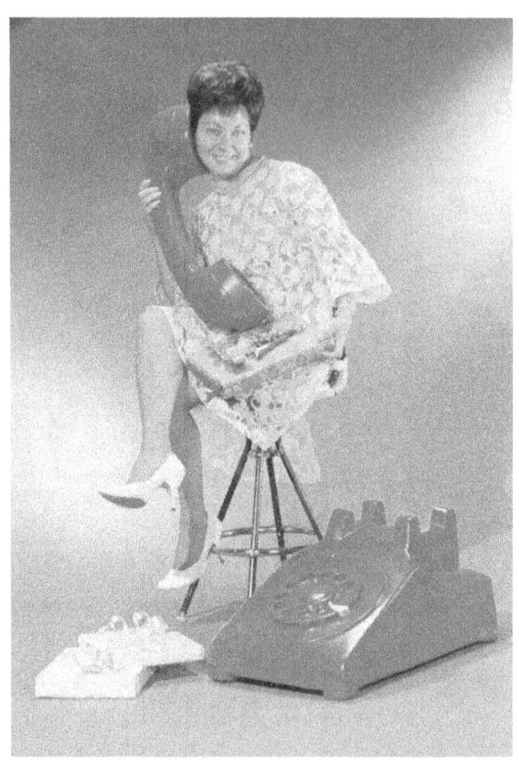

The Maxi-Phone

Tiny telephones that strapped to one's wrist were all the rage until they were supplanted by the even trendier MTIs, or molar telecommunication implants. Sensing that a limit in miniaturization had been reached, Dinklaker Telephony unveiled its Maxi-Phone, a device that was to minuteness what a colonoscopy is to a semicolon.

Uncured

Chiropractor Reg Pringler was head and shoulders above the competition in the back cracking department. His skill at curing neck disorders, however, was questionable at best. Just ask members of the St. Salmons' Comet Spotting Club who, en masse, were recently treated by Dr. Pringler but, sadly, remain as uncured as ham .

Pringlerville Gardens

Pringlerville Gardens, whose ecosystems ranged from cypress swamp to alpine desert, was both one of the foremost botanical gardens in the world and also the biggest vehicle laundering facility. Sure, most visitors were content to simply admire the countless varieties of foliage carefully arranged in a dozen lifelike habitats. But if they drove down any one of a dozen tree-lined corridors at 10 a.m., 2 p.m., or 6:15 p.m., the Gardens' powerful irrigation system would wash their cars sparkling clean! Well, most of the time, anyway.

The Master Camouflager

"I can see you, but you can't see me!" For 16 years, Scooter Dinklaker's boast was incontrovertible. No one *could* see him because the young inventor had turned the art of camouflage into a science. Take the day that he sneaked onto the battlefront of a North African war disguised as a sand dune. As always, no one noticed him – that is, until he inadvertently sneezed, blowing his cover to smithereens. I'd like to report that the nearby troops reacted to his sudden appearance with admirable restraint. Alas, such was not the case.

Sheeplady

Bernice had tried to quit smoking on several occasions, but each time she found that she really missed her little nicotine pick-me-up. That changed when her compromised immune system caused a thick coat of wool to overspread her whole body. She stopped smoking at once, however it was by then too late.

Isabelle Unconvinced

Isabelle was grateful to be playing the starring role of Violetta Valéry in Arnold Dinklaker's production of La Traviata by G.F. Verdi. She simply wasn't convinced that Arnold's vision of moving the venue from an early 18th century Paris salon to the Florida Everglades was the right one, especially with the all too aggressive "props" that Dinklaker had personally donated from his private stock.

Bermuda Triangles

When polled, percussionists of all the major U.S. orchestras said they preferred Bermuda Triangle Company products two to one over other competing brands. Their only complaint was that the instruments, on a regular basis, tended to go missing.

Cecile

After balancing a child on her nose for the umpteenth time that afternoon, Cecile the Seal had had enough. Here she was, a highly intelligent pinniped that could solve complex quadratic equations reduced to performing demeaning circus tricks at county fairs. Well, no more! It was time for her to take control of her life! That was especially unfortunate for Digby and Dolly Dinklaker, who, through no fault of their own, stood next in line and were about to discover just how wrathful a leopard seal could be.

The Aesthetician

Although Bob was now a certified aesthetician, earning him the right to perform lucrative Brazilian bikini body waxes on the city's most beautiful people, he had paid his dues. And in the world of cosmetology, that meant starting with early morning wax jobs on a different and typically unappreciative type of clientele.

Drip Dry

When the always dodgy forced air machine component of the Catalpa Car Wash finally broke down at the start of the busy Father's Day weekend, field manager Darby Dinklaker was forced to quickly come up with an alternative way to dry the vehicles.

The X Note

The X Note is a note that all viola players are taught to avoid. It isn't the highest note in the instrument's repertoire, though it is nearby. Officer Dinklaker here points to the tragic result of a novice violist who played the note. "He'd been warned," Dinklaker says, "but he went ahead and played it anyway."

Specialization

For years, anybody could wash a statute. The labor involved was unskilled—if you had a rag and a bucket of water, you were in business. But then the International Pigeon Roost Society promulgated a set of rules that standardized the cleaning process, sharply steering it towards specialization. That put Bob, who had previously eked out a modest living as an outdoor sculpture maintenance technician, out of a job. But only temporarily. Once he reinvented himself as a Left Nasal Cleansing Consultant and tripled his rates, he found that his services were in demand more than ever.

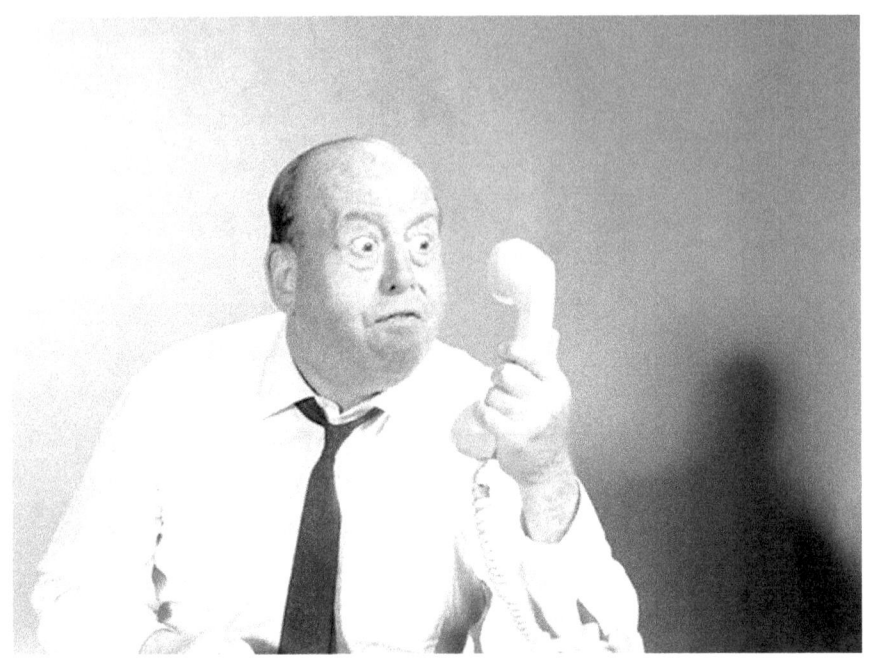

Dial-a-Hypnotist

The number 1 attraction at the recent World Telephony Expo was Dial-A-Hypnotist, a state-of-the-art audio-only mesmerism interface. No matter that respected members of the cognitive-behavior community pooh-poohed the notion that a person can be hypnotized over the phone, user after user swore that it really worked. Bernard, here, would agree, right, Bernard? Uh, Bernard?

Making Do

"If I've told you once I've told you a *hundred* times," said Brenda crossly to her dance partner, Buzz. "Wash the clothes in *cold* water!" It was too late to do anything about it now, so they donned their freshly shrunken costumes for the big supper club fandango finale and just made do.

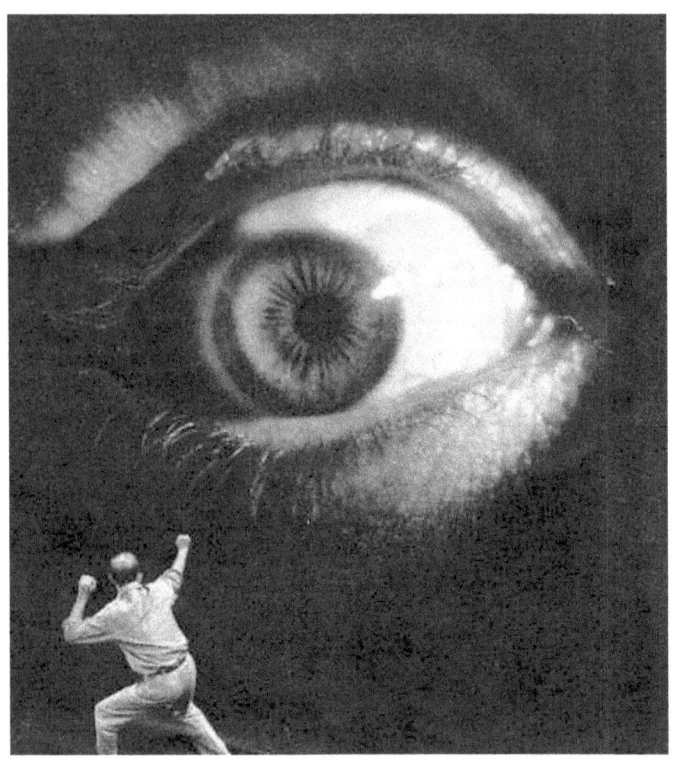

Eye of the Hurricane

Bob was a storm chaser, one of those daring adventurers who seek out extreme weather. But when, one day, he found himself in the eye of a hurricane and the darned thing blinked at him, he forthwith changed his focus to the much less extreme career of optometry.

The Transformation

The Lamington Gallery of Intervallic Art is currently exhibiting a retrospective of the works of photographer Beano Bengaze. One especially remarkable time-lapse image is of Melville Dinklaker as he changes from male to female and back again over the course of thirty hours and half a dozen Jell-O shooters.

Radio Activity

When Pringlerville's constable told the mayor that he had detected radioactivity in Smoodt Memorial Park, the mayor alerted the U.S. Environmental Protection Agency. Within the hour, a HazMat cleanup team had combed the park with Geiger counters, resulting in nothing more than an invoice for 9,000 emergency response dollars, a sum that to this day remains contested by the Pringlerville City Council.

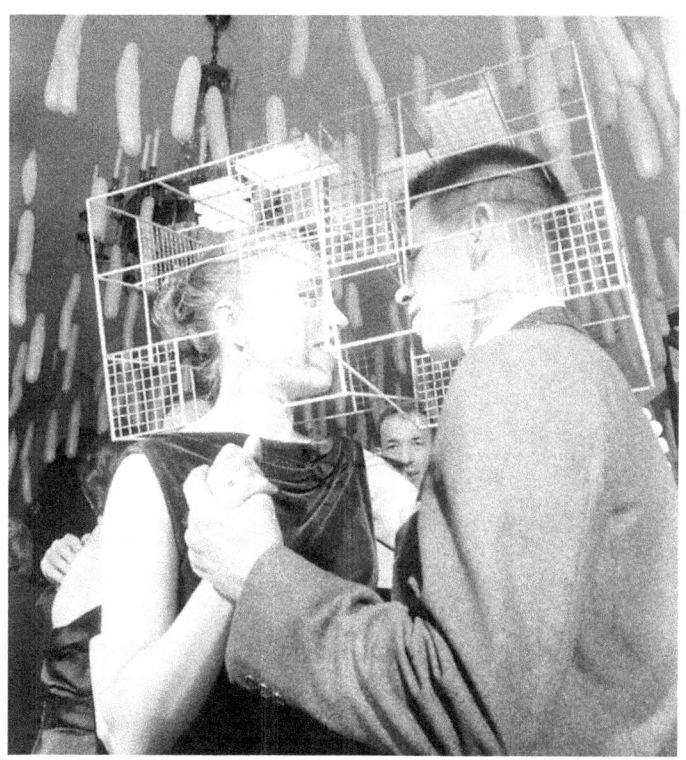

At the Borborygmus Ball

Saint Salmon's Hospital staff were gearing up for their annual fancy dress Borborygmus Ball when a technician discovered a pathogenic French fry in the HVAC system. The hospital commandant promptly cancelled the event, but the resultant hue and cry from the tuberculosis ward patients caused him to reconsider. In the end, he did allow the ball to go on, provided all at-risk attendees wore vector-neutralizing headgear.

Rigor Crus

Plantar fasciitis is a painful inflammation of the eponymous ligament along the bottom of the human foot. In the severe variant known as rigor crus, the leg stiffens to the point of inflexibility. Curiously, rigor crus is also contagious.

Lilliputitis

When Gulliver returned to England after vacationing on Lilliput Island, he unwittingly brought back a virulent strain of Lilliputisis, a disease that renders its victim diminutive, though without attenuating her or his appetite. Fortunately, the malady can be reversed in patients who eat the flowers of *Brobdingnagolos shrubulum*, an ornamental bush to which Blanche, pictured, unfortunately does not have access.

Mascaraman

With his superpowers limited to possessing an alarming countenance, it wasn't surprising that Mascaraman was one of Guardians of the Galaxy's more overlooked members.

The Soothsayer

General Wilbur "Shorty" Dinklaker was renowned for his wartime foresight. Time after time, he predicted a military conflict's outcome with uncanny accuracy. But Dinklaker's prognosticating success was due solely to his friend, Phil, who was a soothsayer. And Phil's allegiance to the general was due to Annette, Dinklaker's comely aide-de-camp. Sadly, the arrangement fell apart one day in early December when Phil came out of his prophetical trance prematurely and caught Wilbur and Annette making goo-goo eyes at each other. He sensed correctly that some hanky-panky had been going on for some time, too. *The heck with national security!*, he muttered as he stormed off in a huff, never to return. The next day, December 7, 1941 – well, you probably already know what happened.

About Fomite

A fomite is a medium capable of transmitting infectious organisms from one individual to another.

"The activity of art is based on the capacity of people to be infected by the feelings of others." Tolstoy, *What Is Art?*

Writing a review on Amazon, Good Reads, Shelfari, Library Thing or other social media sites for readers will help the progress of independent publishing. To submit a review, go to the book page on any of the sites and follow the links for reviews. Books from independent presses rely on reader to reader communications.

For more information or to order any of our books, visit http://www.fomitepress.com/FOMITE/Our_Books.html

More Titles from Fomite...

Novels
Joshua Amses — *During This, Our Nadir*
Joshua Amses — *Raven or Crow*
Joshua Amses — *The Moment Before an Injury*
Jaysinh Birjepatel — *The Good Muslim of Jackson Heights*
Jaysinh Birjepatel — *Nothing Beside Remains*
David Brizer — *Victor Rand*
Paula Closson Buck — *Summer on the Cold War Planet*
Marc Estrin — *Hyde*
Marc Estrin — *Speckled Vanitie*
Zdravka Evtimova — *Sinfonia Bulgarica*
Daniel Forbes — *Derail This Train Wreck*
Greg Guma — *Dons of Time*
Richard Hawley — *The Three Lives of Jonathan Force*
Lamar Herrin — *Father Figure*
Ron Jacobs — *All the Sinners Saints*

Fomite

Ron Jacobs — *Short Order Frame Up*
Ron Jacobs — *The Co-conspirator's Tale*
Scott Archer Jones — *A Rising Tide of People Swept Away*
Maggie Kast — *A Free Unsullied Land*
Darrell Kastin — *Shadowboxing with Bukowski*
Coleen Kearon — *Feminist on Fire*
Jan Englis Leary — *Thicker Than Blood*
Diane Lefer — *Confessions of a Carnivore*
Rob Lenihan — *Born Speaking Lies*
Ilan Mochari — *Zinsky the Obscure*
Andy Potok — *My Father's Keeper*
Robert Rosenberg — *Isles of the Blind*
Fred Skolnik — *Rafi's World*
Lynn Sloan — *Principles of Navigation*
L.E. Smith — *The Consequence of Gesture*
L.E. Smith — *Travers' Inferno*
Bob Sommer — *A Great Fullness*
Tom Walker — *A Day in the Life*
Susan V. Weiss — *My God, What Have We Done?*
Peter M. Wheelwright — *As It Is On Earth*
Suzie Wizowaty — *The Return of Jason Green*

Poetry
Antonello Borra — *Alfabestiario*
Antonello Borra — *AlphaBetaBestiaro*
James Connolly — *Picking Up the Bodies*
Greg Delanty — *Loosestrife*
Mason Drukman — *Drawing on Life*
J. C. Ellefson — *Foreign Tales of Exemplum and Woe*
Anna Faktorovich — *Improvisational Arguments*
Barry Goldensohn — *Snake in the Spine, Wolf in the Heart*
Barry Goldensohn — *The Hundred Yard Dash Man*
Barry Goldensohn — *The Listener Aspires to the Condition of Music*
R. L. Green When — *You Remember Deir Yassin*
Kate Magill — *Roadworthy Creature, Roadworthy Craft*
Tony Magistrale — *Entanglements*

Fomite

Sherry Olson — *Four-Way Stop*
Janice Miller Potter — *Meanwell*
Joseph D. Reich — *Connecting the Dots to Shangrila*
Joseph D. Reich — *The Hole That Runs Through Utopia*
Joseph D. Reich — *The Housing Market*
Joseph D. Reich — *The Derivation of Cowboys and Indians*
David Schein — *My Murder and Other Local News*
Scott T. Starbuck — *Industrial Oz*
Seth Steinzor — *Among the Lost*
Seth Steinzor — *To Join the Lost*
Susan Thomas — *The Empty Notebook Interrogates Itself*
Sharon Webster — *Everyone Lives Here*
Tony Whedon — *The Tres Riches Heures*
Tony Whedon — *The Falkland Quartet*

Stories
Jay Boyer — *Flight*
Michael Cocchiarale — *Still Time*
Neil Connelly — *In the Wake of Our Vows*
Catherine Zobal Dent — *Unfinished Stories of Girls*
Zdravka Evtimova —*Carts and Other Stories*
John Michael Flynn — *Off to the Next Wherever*
Elizabeth Genovise — *Where There Are Two or More*
Andrei Guriuanu — *Body of Work*
Derek Furr — *Semitones*
Derek Furr — *Suite for Three Voices*
Zeke Jarvis — *In A Family Way*
Marjorie Maddox — *What She Was Saying*
William Marquess — *Boom-shacka-lacka*
Gary Miller — *Museum of the Americas*
Jennifer Anne Moses — *Visiting Hours*
Martin Ott — *Interrogations*
Jack Pulaski — *Love's Labours*
Charles Rafferty — *Saturday Night at Magellan's*
Kathryn Roberts — *Companion Plants*
Ron Savage — *What We Do For Love*

L.E. Smith — *Views Cost Extra*
Susan Thomas — *Among Angelic Orders*
Tom Walker — *Signed Confessions*
Silas Dent Zobal — *The Inconvenience of the Wings*

Odd Birds
Micheal Breiner — *the way none of this happened*
Gail Holst-Warhaft — *The Fall of Athens*
Roger Leboitz — *A Guide to the Western Slopes and the Outlying Area*
dug Nap— *Artsy Fartsy*
Delia Bell Robinson — *A Shirtwaist Story*
Peter Schumann — *Planet Kasper, Volumes One and Two*
Peter Schumann — *Bread & Sentences*
Peter Schumann — *Faust 3*

Plays
Stephen Goldberg — *Screwed and Other Plays*
Michele Markarian — *Unborn Children of America*

www.ingramcontent.com/pod-product-compliance
Lightning Source LLC
Chambersburg PA
CBHW071734080526
44588CB00013B/2030